MW00933455

THIS BOOK BELONGS TO

_____

HIKING CHECKLIST

CLOTHING

- [ ] HIKING BOOTS
- [ ] WOOL SOCKS
- [ ] BASE LAYERS
- [ ] SHORT SLEEVED SHIRT
- [ ] LONG SLEEVED SHIRT
- [ ] INSULATED MIDLAYER
- [ ] SUN HAT / VISOR
- [ ] BANDANA
- [ ] RAINWEAR
- [ ] WATCH

EQUIPMENT

- [ ] MAP
- [ ] COMPASS
- [ ] FLASHLIGHT
- [ ] HEAD LAMP
- [ ] LIGHTER / MATCHES
- [ ] KNIFE / MULTI-TOOL
- [ ] CELL PHONE
- [ ] POUCH
- [ ] MOLESKIN
- [ ] TREKKING POLES

FOOD & SUPPLIES

- [ ] MEALS & SNACKS
- [ ] WATER BOTTLE
- [ ] WATER TREATMENT
- [ ] COOKING POT
- [ ] COOKSTOVE/FUEL
- [ ] EATING UTENSILS
- [ ] BOWL/MUG/PLATE
- [ ] GARBAGE BAGS
- [ ] ROPE
- [ ] FOLDABLE BUCKET

CAMPING GEAR

- [ ] TENT
- [ ] SLEEPING BAG
- [ ] SLEEPING PAD
- [ ] TOILET PAPER
- [ ] BACKPACK
- [ ] DUCT TAPE
- [ ] FOLDING SAW
- [ ] POT LIFTER
- [ ] CAMP SHOES
- [ ] BEAR BANGER

MISC.

- [ ] INSECT REPELLENT
- [ ] LIP BALM
- [ ] FACE PROTECTOR
- [ ] EXTRA GLOVES
- [ ] DEODORANT
- [ ] HEADPHONES
- [ ] BATTERIES
- [ ] CHARGER
- [ ] DECK OF CARDS
- [ ] GPS

OTHER

- [ ] _____
- [ ] _____
- [ ] _____
- [ ] _____
- [ ] _____
- [ ] _____
- [ ] _____
- [ ] _____
- [ ] _____
- [ ] _____

HIKING CHECKLIST

CLOTHING

- [ ] HIKING BOOTS
- [ ] WOOL SOCKS
- [ ] BASE LAYERS
- [ ] SHORT SLEEVED SHIRT
- [ ] LONG SLEEVED SHIRT
- [ ] INSULATED MIDLAYER
- [ ] SUN HAT / VISOR
- [ ] BANDANA
- [ ] RAINWEAR
- [ ] WATCH

EQUIPMENT

- [ ] MAP
- [ ] COMPASS
- [ ] FLASHLIGHT
- [ ] HEAD LAMP
- [ ] LIGHTER / MATCHES
- [ ] KNIFE / MULTI-TOOL
- [ ] CELL PHONE
- [ ] POUCH
- [ ] MOLESKIN
- [ ] TREKKING POLES

FOOD & SUPPLIES

- [ ] MEALS & SNACKS
- [ ] WATER BOTTLE
- [ ] WATER TREATMENT
- [ ] COOKING POT
- [ ] COOKSTOVE/FUEL
- [ ] EATING UTENSILS
- [ ] BOWL/MUG/PLATE
- [ ] GARBAGE BAGS
- [ ] ROPE
- [ ] FOLDABLE BUCKET

CAMPING GEAR

- [ ] TENT
- [ ] SLEEPING BAG
- [ ] SLEEPING PAD
- [ ] TOILET PAPER
- [ ] BACKPACK
- [ ] DUCT TAPE
- [ ] FOLDING SAW
- [ ] POT LIFTER
- [ ] CAMP SHOES
- [ ] BEAR BANGER

MISC.

- [ ] INSECT REPELLENT
- [ ] LIP BALM
- [ ] FACE PROTECTOR
- [ ] EXTRA GLOVES
- [ ] DEODORANT
- [ ] HEADPHONES
- [ ] BATTERIES
- [ ] CHARGER
- [ ] DECK OF CARDS
- [ ] GPS

OTHER

- [ ] _____
- [ ] _____
- [ ] _____
- [ ] _____
- [ ] _____
- [ ] _____
- [ ] _____
- [ ] _____
- [ ] _____
- [ ] _____

HIKING CHECKLIST

CLOTHING

- HIKING BOOTS
- WOOL SOCKS
- BASE LAYERS
- SHORT SLEEVED SHIRT
- LONG SLEEVED SHIRT
- INSULATED MIDLAYER
- SUN HAT / VISOR
- BANDANA
- RAINWEAR
- WATCH

EQUIPMENT

- MAP
- COMPASS
- FLASHLIGHT
- HEAD LAMP
- LIGHTER / MATCHES
- KNIFE / MULTI-TOOL
- CELL PHONE
- POUCH
- MOLESKIN
- TREKKING POLES

FOOD & SUPPLIES

- MEALS & SNACKS
- WATER BOTTLE
- WATER TREATMENT
- COOKING POT
- COOKSTOVE/FUEL
- EATING UTENSILS
- BOWL/MUG/PLATE
- GARBAGE BAGS
- ROPE
- FOLDABLE BUCKET

CAMPING GEAR

- TENT
- SLEEPING BAG
- SLEEPING PAD
- TOILET PAPER
- BACKPACK
- DUCT TAPE
- FOLDING SAW
- POT LIFTER
- CAMP SHOES
- BEAR BANGER

MISC.

- INSECT REPELLENT
- LIP BALM
- FACE PROTECTOR
- EXTRA GLOVES
- DEODORANT
- HEADPHONES
- BATTERIES
- CHARGER
- DECK OF CARDS
- GPS

OTHER

- _____
- _____
- _____
- _____
- _____
- _____
- _____
- _____
- _____
- _____

HIKING CHECKLIST

CLOTHING

- [ ] HIKING BOOTS
- [ ] WOOL SOCKS
- [ ] BASE LAYERS
- [ ] SHORT SLEEVED SHIRT
- [ ] LONG SLEEVED SHIRT
- [ ] INSULATED MIDLAYER
- [ ] SUN HAT / VISOR
- [ ] BANDANA
- [ ] RAINWEAR
- [ ] WATCH

EQUIPMENT

- [ ] MAP
- [ ] COMPASS
- [ ] FLASHLIGHT
- [ ] HEAD LAMP
- [ ] LIGHTER / MATCHES
- [ ] KNIFE / MULTI-TOOL
- [ ] CELL PHONE
- [ ] POUCH
- [ ] MOLESKIN
- [ ] TREKKING POLES

FOOD & SUPPLIES

- [ ] MEALS & SNACKS
- [ ] WATER BOTTLE
- [ ] WATER TREATMENT
- [ ] COOKING POT
- [ ] COOKSTOVE/FUEL
- [ ] EATING UTENSILS
- [ ] BOWL/MUG/PLATE
- [ ] GARBAGE BAGS
- [ ] ROPE
- [ ] FOLDABLE BUCKET

CAMPING GEAR

- [ ] TENT
- [ ] SLEEPING BAG
- [ ] SLEEPING PAD
- [ ] TOILET PAPER
- [ ] BACKPACK
- [ ] DUCT TAPE
- [ ] FOLDING SAW
- [ ] POT LIFTER
- [ ] CAMP SHOES
- [ ] BEAR BANGER

MISC.

- [ ] INSECT REPELLENT
- [ ] LIP BALM
- [ ] FACE PROTECTOR
- [ ] EXTRA GLOVES
- [ ] DEODORANT
- [ ] HEADPHONES
- [ ] BATTERIES
- [ ] CHARGER
- [ ] DECK OF CARDS
- [ ] GPS

OTHER

- [ ] _____
- [ ] _____
- [ ] _____
- [ ] _____
- [ ] _____
- [ ] _____
- [ ] _____
- [ ] _____
- [ ] _____
- [ ] _____

HIKING LOGBOOK

DATE

RATING: ☆☆☆☆☆

TRAIL	ELEVATION GAIN	LOSS
LOCATION		

DISTANCE	DURATION	START TIME	END TIME

TRAIL TYPE	DIFFICULTY	WEATHER

IMPORTANT TRAIL DETAILS	OBSERVANCES (views, nature, wildlife…)

TRAIL SURFACE	EXPOSURE	NOTES FOR NEXT TIME

HIKING NOTES

ADVENTURE
is
calling

HIKING LOGBOOK

DATE:

RATING: ☆☆☆☆☆

TRAIL	ELEVATION GAIN	LOSS
LOCATION		

DISTANCE	DURATION	START TIME	END TIME

TRAIL TYPE	DIFFICULTY	WEATHER

IMPORTANT TRAIL DETAILS	OBSERVANCES (views, nature, wildlife…)

TRAIL SURFACE	EXPOSURE	NOTES FOR NEXT TIME

HIKING NOTES

ADVENTURE
awaits

HIKING LOGBOOK

DATE: RATING: ☆☆☆☆☆

TRAIL	ELEVATION GAIN	LOSS
LOCATION		

DISTANCE	DURATION	START TIME	END TIME

TRAIL TYPE	DIFFICULTY	WEATHER

IMPORTANT TRAIL DETAILS	OBSERVANCES (views, nature, wildlife...)

TRAIL SURFACE	EXPOSURE	NOTES FOR NEXT TIME

HIKING NOTES

HIKING LOGBOOK

DATE: RATING: ☆☆☆☆☆

TRAIL	ELEVATION GAIN	LOSS
LOCATION		

DISTANCE	DURATION	START TIME	END TIME

TRAIL TYPE	DIFFICULTY	WEATHER	

IMPORTANT TRAIL DETAILS	OBSERVANCES (views, nature, wildlife...)

TRAIL SURFACE	EXPOSURE	NOTES FOR NEXT TIME

HIKING NOTES

HIKING LOGBOOK

DATE

RATING: ☆☆☆☆☆

TRAIL	ELEVATION GAIN	LOSS
LOCATION		

DISTANCE	DURATION	START TIME	END TIME

TRAIL TYPE	DIFFICULTY	WEATHER

IMPORTANT TRAIL DETAILS	OBSERVANCES (views, nature, wildlife...)

TRAIL SURFACE	EXPOSURE	NOTES FOR NEXT TIME

HIKING NOTES

ADVENTURE
is
calling

HIKING LOGBOOK

DATE: RATING: ☆☆☆☆☆

TRAIL	ELEVATION GAIN	LOSS
LOCATION		

DISTANCE	DURATION	START TIME	END TIME

TRAIL TYPE	DIFFICULTY	WEATHER

IMPORTANT TRAIL DETAILS	OBSERVANCES (views, nature, wildlife…)

TRAIL SURFACE	EXPOSURE	NOTES FOR NEXT TIME

HIKING NOTES

ADVENTURE
awaits

HIKING LOGBOOK

DATE: RATING: ☆☆☆☆☆

TRAIL	ELEVATION GAIN	LOSS
LOCATION		

DISTANCE	DURATION	START TIME	END TIME

TRAIL TYPE	DIFFICULTY	WEATHER

IMPORTANT TRAIL DETAILS	OBSERVANCES (views, nature, wildlife…)

TRAIL SURFACE	EXPOSURE	NOTES FOR NEXT TIME

HIKING NOTES

HIKING LOGBOOK

DATE: RATING: ☆☆☆☆☆

TRAIL	ELEVATION GAIN	LOSS
LOCATION		

DISTANCE	DURATION	START TIME	END TIME

TRAIL TYPE	DIFFICULTY	WEATHER

IMPORTANT TRAIL DETAILS	OBSERVANCES (views, nature, wildlife…)

TRAIL SURFACE	EXPOSURE	NOTES FOR NEXT TIME

HIKING NOTES

HIKING LOGBOOK

DATE

RATING: ☆☆☆☆☆

TRAIL	ELEVATION GAIN	LOSS
LOCATION		

DISTANCE	DURATION	START TIME	END TIME

TRAIL TYPE	DIFFICULTY	WEATHER

IMPORTANT TRAIL DETAILS	OBSERVANCES (views, nature, wildlife...)

TRAIL SURFACE	EXPOSURE	NOTES FOR NEXT TIME

HIKING NOTES

ADVENTURE
is
calling

HIKING LOGBOOK

DATE: RATING: ☆☆☆☆☆

TRAIL	ELEVATION GAIN	LOSS
LOCATION		

DISTANCE	DURATION	START TIME	END TIME

TRAIL TYPE	DIFFICULTY	WEATHER

IMPORTANT TRAIL DETAILS	OBSERVANCES (views, nature, wildlife...)

TRAIL SURFACE	EXPOSURE	NOTES FOR NEXT TIME

HIKING NOTES

ADVENTURE
awaits

HIKING LOGBOOK

DATE: RATING: ☆ ☆ ☆ ☆ ☆

TRAIL		ELEVATION GAIN	LOSS
LOCATION			

DISTANCE	DURATION	START TIME	END TIME

TRAIL TYPE	DIFFICULTY	WEATHER	

IMPORTANT TRAIL DETAILS		OBSERVANCES (views, nature, wildlife…)	

TRAIL SURFACE	EXPOSURE	NOTES FOR NEXT TIME	

HIKING NOTES

HIKING LOGBOOK

DATE:

RATING: ☆☆☆☆☆

TRAIL	ELEVATION GAIN	LOSS
LOCATION		

DISTANCE	DURATION	START TIME	END TIME

TRAIL TYPE	DIFFICULTY	WEATHER

IMPORTANT TRAIL DETAILS	OBSERVANCES (views, nature, wildlife...)

TRAIL SURFACE	EXPOSURE	NOTES FOR NEXT TIME

HIKING NOTES

HIKING LOGBOOK

DATE

RATING: ☆☆☆☆☆

TRAIL	ELEVATION GAIN	LOSS
LOCATION		

DISTANCE	DURATION	START TIME	END TIME

TRAIL TYPE	DIFFICULTY	WEATHER

IMPORTANT TRAIL DETAILS	OBSERVANCES (views, nature, wildlife...)

TRAIL SURFACE	EXPOSURE	NOTES FOR NEXT TIME

HIKING NOTES

ADVENTURE
is
calling

HIKING LOGBOOK

DATE:

RATING: ☆☆☆☆☆

TRAIL	ELEVATION GAIN	LOSS
LOCATION		

DISTANCE	DURATION	START TIME	END TIME

TRAIL TYPE	DIFFICULTY	WEATHER

IMPORTANT TRAIL DETAILS	OBSERVANCES (views, nature, wildlife...)

TRAIL SURFACE	EXPOSURE	NOTES FOR NEXT TIME

HIKING NOTES

ADVENTURE
awaits

HIKING LOGBOOK

DATE:

RATING: ☆☆☆☆☆

TRAIL	ELEVATION GAIN	LOSS
LOCATION		

DISTANCE	DURATION	START TIME	END TIME

TRAIL TYPE	DIFFICULTY	WEATHER

IMPORTANT TRAIL DETAILS	OBSERVANCES (views, nature, wildlife...)

TRAIL SURFACE	EXPOSURE	NOTES FOR NEXT TIME

HIKING NOTES

HIKING LOGBOOK

DATE: RATING: ☆ ☆ ☆ ☆ ☆

TRAIL	ELEVATION GAIN	LOSS
LOCATION		

DISTANCE	DURATION	START TIME	END TIME

TRAIL TYPE	DIFFICULTY	WEATHER

IMPORTANT TRAIL DETAILS	OBSERVANCES (views, nature, wildlife…)

TRAIL SURFACE	EXPOSURE	NOTES FOR NEXT TIME

HIKING NOTES

HIKING LOGBOOK

DATE

RATING: ☆☆☆☆☆

TRAIL	ELEVATION GAIN	LOSS
LOCATION		

DISTANCE	DURATION	START TIME	END TIME

TRAIL TYPE	DIFFICULTY	WEATHER	

IMPORTANT TRAIL DETAILS

OBSERVANCES (views, nature, wildlife...)

TRAIL SURFACE	EXPOSURE	NOTES FOR NEXT TIME

HIKING NOTES

ADVENTURE
is
calling

HIKING LOGBOOK

DATE: RATING: ☆ ☆ ☆ ☆ ☆

TRAIL	ELEVATION GAIN	LOSS
LOCATION		

DISTANCE	DURATION	START TIME	END TIME

TRAIL TYPE	DIFFICULTY	WEATHER	

IMPORTANT TRAIL DETAILS		OBSERVANCES (views, nature, wildlife...)	

TRAIL SURFACE	EXPOSURE	NOTES FOR NEXT TIME	

HIKING NOTES

ADVENTURE
awaits

HIKING LOGBOOK

DATE: RATING: ☆☆☆☆☆

TRAIL	ELEVATION GAIN	LOSS
LOCATION		

DISTANCE	DURATION	START TIME	END TIME

TRAIL TYPE	DIFFICULTY	WEATHER

IMPORTANT TRAIL DETAILS	OBSERVANCES (views, nature, wildlife…)

TRAIL SURFACE	EXPOSURE	NOTES FOR NEXT TIME

HIKING NOTES

HIKING LOGBOOK

DATE: RATING: ☆☆☆☆☆

TRAIL	ELEVATION GAIN	LOSS
LOCATION		

DISTANCE	DURATION	START TIME	END TIME

TRAIL TYPE	DIFFICULTY	WEATHER

IMPORTANT TRAIL DETAILS	OBSERVANCES (views, nature, wildlife…)

TRAIL SURFACE	EXPOSURE	NOTES FOR NEXT TIME

HIKING NOTES

_____

_____

_____

_____

_____

_____

_____

_____

_____

_____

_____

_____

_____

_____

_____

_____

_____

HIKING LOGBOOK

DATE   RATING: ☆☆☆☆☆

TRAIL		ELEVATION GAIN	LOSS
LOCATION			

DISTANCE	DURATION	START TIME	END TIME

TRAIL TYPE	DIFFICULTY	WEATHER	

IMPORTANT TRAIL DETAILS	OBSERVANCES (views, nature, wildlife...)

TRAIL SURFACE	EXPOSURE	NOTES FOR NEXT TIME

HIKING NOTES

ADVENTURE
~IS~
calling

_____

_____

_____

_____

_____

_____

_____

_____

_____

_____

_____

_____

_____

_____

_____

_____

HIKING LOGBOOK

DATE: RATING: ☆☆☆☆☆

TRAIL	ELEVATION GAIN	LOSS
LOCATION		

DISTANCE	DURATION	START TIME	END TIME

TRAIL TYPE	DIFFICULTY	WEATHER	

IMPORTANT TRAIL DETAILS	OBSERVANCES (views, nature, wildlife...)

TRAIL SURFACE	EXPOSURE	NOTES FOR NEXT TIME

HIKING NOTES

ADVENTURE
awaits

HIKING LOGBOOK

DATE: RATING: ☆☆☆☆☆

TRAIL	ELEVATION GAIN	LOSS
LOCATION		

DISTANCE	DURATION	START TIME	END TIME

TRAIL TYPE	DIFFICULTY	WEATHER

IMPORTANT TRAIL DETAILS	OBSERVANCES (views, nature, wildlife…)

TRAIL SURFACE	EXPOSURE	NOTES FOR NEXT TIME

HIKING NOTES

HIKING LOGBOOK

DATE: RATING: ☆☆☆☆☆

TRAIL	ELEVATION GAIN	LOSS
LOCATION		

DISTANCE	DURATION	START TIME	END TIME

TRAIL TYPE	DIFFICULTY	WEATHER

IMPORTANT TRAIL DETAILS	OBSERVANCES (views, nature, wildlife...)

TRAIL SURFACE	EXPOSURE	NOTES FOR NEXT TIME

HIKING NOTES

HIKING LOGBOOK

DATE

RATING: ☆☆☆☆☆

TRAIL	ELEVATION GAIN	LOSS
LOCATION		

DISTANCE	DURATION	START TIME	END TIME

TRAIL TYPE	DIFFICULTY	WEATHER	

IMPORTANT TRAIL DETAILS		OBSERVANCES (views, nature, wildlife...)	

TRAIL SURFACE	EXPOSURE	NOTES FOR NEXT TIME	

HIKING NOTES

ADVENTURE
is
calling

HIKING LOGBOOK

DATE: RATING: ☆☆☆☆☆

TRAIL	ELEVATION GAIN	LOSS
LOCATION		

DISTANCE	DURATION	START TIME	END TIME

TRAIL TYPE	DIFFICULTY	WEATHER	

IMPORTANT TRAIL DETAILS		OBSERVANCES (views, nature, wildlife…)	

TRAIL SURFACE	EXPOSURE	NOTES FOR NEXT TIME	

HIKING NOTES

ADVENTURE awaits

HIKING LOGBOOK

DATE: RATING: ☆☆☆☆☆

TRAIL	ELEVATION GAIN	LOSS
LOCATION		

DISTANCE	DURATION	START TIME	END TIME

TRAIL TYPE	DIFFICULTY	WEATHER	

IMPORTANT TRAIL DETAILS		OBSERVANCES (views, nature, wildlife...)	

TRAIL SURFACE	EXPOSURE	NOTES FOR NEXT TIME	

HIKING NOTES

HIKING LOGBOOK

DATE: _____   RATING: ☆ ☆ ☆ ☆ ☆

TRAIL	ELEVATION GAIN	LOSS
LOCATION		

DISTANCE	DURATION	START TIME	END TIME

TRAIL TYPE	DIFFICULTY	WEATHER

IMPORTANT TRAIL DETAILS	OBSERVANCES (views, nature, wildlife...)

TRAIL SURFACE	EXPOSURE	NOTES FOR NEXT TIME

HIKING NOTES

HIKING LOGBOOK

DATE

RATING: ☆☆☆☆☆

TRAIL	ELEVATION GAIN	LOSS
LOCATION		

DISTANCE	DURATION	START TIME	END TIME

TRAIL TYPE	DIFFICULTY	WEATHER

IMPORTANT TRAIL DETAILS	OBSERVANCES (views, nature, wildlife...)

TRAIL SURFACE	EXPOSURE	NOTES FOR NEXT TIME

HIKING NOTES

ADVENTURE
is
calling

HIKING LOGBOOK

DATE: RATING: ☆☆☆☆☆

TRAIL	ELEVATION GAIN	LOSS
LOCATION		

DISTANCE	DURATION	START TIME	END TIME

TRAIL TYPE	DIFFICULTY	WEATHER

IMPORTANT TRAIL DETAILS	OBSERVANCES (views, nature, wildlife...)

TRAIL SURFACE	EXPOSURE	NOTES FOR NEXT TIME

HIKING NOTES

ADVENTURE
awaits

HIKING LOGBOOK

DATE: RATING: ☆☆☆☆☆

TRAIL	ELEVATION GAIN	LOSS
LOCATION		

DISTANCE	DURATION	START TIME	END TIME

TRAIL TYPE	DIFFICULTY	WEATHER	

IMPORTANT TRAIL DETAILS	OBSERVANCES (views, nature, wildlife...)

TRAIL SURFACE	EXPOSURE	NOTES FOR NEXT TIME

HIKING NOTES

HIKING LOGBOOK

DATE: RATING: ☆☆☆☆☆

TRAIL		ELEVATION GAIN	LOSS
LOCATION			

DISTANCE	DURATION	START TIME	END TIME

TRAIL TYPE	DIFFICULTY	WEATHER	

IMPORTANT TRAIL DETAILS		OBSERVANCES (views, nature, wildlife…)	

TRAIL SURFACE	EXPOSURE	NOTES FOR NEXT TIME	

HIKING NOTES

HIKING LOGBOOK

DATE

RATING: ☆☆☆☆☆

TRAIL

ELEVATION GAIN

LOSS

LOCATION

DISTANCE

DURATION

START TIME

END TIME

TRAIL TYPE

DIFFICULTY

WEATHER

IMPORTANT TRAIL DETAILS

OBSERVANCES (views, nature, wildlife...)

TRAIL SURFACE

EXPOSURE

NOTES FOR NEXT TIME

HIKING NOTES

ADVENTURE
is
calling

HIKING LOGBOOK

DATE: RATING: ☆☆☆☆☆

TRAIL	ELEVATION GAIN	LOSS
LOCATION		

DISTANCE	DURATION	START TIME	END TIME

TRAIL TYPE	DIFFICULTY	WEATHER	

IMPORTANT TRAIL DETAILS	OBSERVANCES (views, nature, wildlife…)

TRAIL SURFACE	EXPOSURE	NOTES FOR NEXT TIME

HIKING NOTES

ADVENTURE
awaits

HIKING LOGBOOK

DATE: RATING: ☆☆☆☆☆

TRAIL	ELEVATION GAIN	LOSS
LOCATION		

DISTANCE	DURATION	START TIME	END TIME

TRAIL TYPE	DIFFICULTY	WEATHER	

IMPORTANT TRAIL DETAILS		OBSERVANCES (views, nature, wildlife…)	

TRAIL SURFACE	EXPOSURE	NOTES FOR NEXT TIME	

HIKING NOTES

HIKING LOGBOOK

DATE: RATING: ☆☆☆☆☆

TRAIL	ELEVATION GAIN	LOSS
LOCATION		

DISTANCE	DURATION	START TIME	END TIME

TRAIL TYPE	DIFFICULTY	WEATHER

IMPORTANT TRAIL DETAILS	OBSERVANCES (views, nature, wildlife…)

TRAIL SURFACE	EXPOSURE	NOTES FOR NEXT TIME

HIKING NOTES

HIKING LOGBOOK

DATE

RATING: ☆☆☆☆☆

TRAIL

ELEVATION GAIN

LOSS

LOCATION

DISTANCE

DURATION

START TIME

END TIME

TRAIL TYPE

DIFFICULTY

WEATHER

IMPORTANT TRAIL DETAILS

OBSERVANCES (views, nature, wildlife...)

TRAIL SURFACE

EXPOSURE

NOTES FOR NEXT TIME

HIKING NOTES

ADVENTURE
is
calling

HIKING LOGBOOK

DATE: RATING: ☆☆☆☆☆

TRAIL	ELEVATION GAIN	LOSS
LOCATION		

DISTANCE	DURATION	START TIME	END TIME

TRAIL TYPE	DIFFICULTY	WEATHER

IMPORTANT TRAIL DETAILS	OBSERVANCES (views, nature, wildlife...)

TRAIL SURFACE	EXPOSURE	NOTES FOR NEXT TIME

HIKING NOTES

HIKING LOGBOOK

DATE:

RATING: ☆☆☆☆☆

TRAIL		ELEVATION GAIN	LOSS
LOCATION			

DISTANCE	DURATION	START TIME	END TIME

TRAIL TYPE	DIFFICULTY	WEATHER

IMPORTANT TRAIL DETAILS	OBSERVANCES (views, nature, wildlife...)

TRAIL SURFACE	EXPOSURE	NOTES FOR NEXT TIME

HIKING NOTES

_____

_____

_____

_____

_____

_____

_____

_____

_____

_____

_____

_____

_____

_____

_____

_____

_____

_____

HIKING LOGBOOK

DATE: RATING: ☆ ☆ ☆ ☆ ☆

TRAIL		ELEVATION GAIN	LOSS
LOCATION			
DISTANCE	DURATION	START TIME	END TIME
TRAIL TYPE	DIFFICULTY	WEATHER	
IMPORTANT TRAIL DETAILS		OBSERVANCES (views, nature, wildlife...)	
TRAIL SURFACE	EXPOSURE	NOTES FOR NEXT TIME	

HIKING NOTES

HIKING LOGBOOK

DATE

RATING: ☆☆☆☆☆

TRAIL	ELEVATION GAIN	LOSS
LOCATION		

DISTANCE	DURATION	START TIME	END TIME

TRAIL TYPE	DIFFICULTY	WEATHER

IMPORTANT TRAIL DETAILS	OBSERVANCES (views, nature, wildlife...)

TRAIL SURFACE	EXPOSURE	NOTES FOR NEXT TIME

HIKING NOTES

ADVENTURE
is
calling

HIKING LOGBOOK

DATE: RATING: ☆☆☆☆☆

TRAIL	ELEVATION GAIN	LOSS
LOCATION		

DISTANCE	DURATION	START TIME	END TIME

TRAIL TYPE	DIFFICULTY	WEATHER	

IMPORTANT TRAIL DETAILS		OBSERVANCES (views, nature, wildlife…)	

TRAIL SURFACE	EXPOSURE	NOTES FOR NEXT TIME	

HIKING NOTES

ADVENTURE
awaits

HIKING LOGBOOK

DATE: RATING: ☆ ☆ ☆ ☆ ☆

TRAIL	ELEVATION GAIN	LOSS
LOCATION		

DISTANCE	DURATION	START TIME	END TIME

TRAIL TYPE	DIFFICULTY	WEATHER

IMPORTANT TRAIL DETAILS	OBSERVANCES (views, nature, wildlife...)

TRAIL SURFACE	EXPOSURE	NOTES FOR NEXT TIME

HIKING NOTES

HIKING LOGBOOK

DATE: RATING: ☆☆☆☆☆

TRAIL	ELEVATION GAIN	LOSS
LOCATION		

DISTANCE	DURATION	START TIME	END TIME

TRAIL TYPE	DIFFICULTY	WEATHER	

IMPORTANT TRAIL DETAILS		OBSERVANCES (views, nature, wildlife…)	

TRAIL SURFACE	EXPOSURE	NOTES FOR NEXT TIME	

HIKING NOTES

HIKING LOGBOOK

DATE

RATING: ☆☆☆☆☆

TRAIL

ELEVATION GAIN

LOSS

LOCATION

DISTANCE

DURATION

START TIME

END TIME

TRAIL TYPE

DIFFICULTY

WEATHER

IMPORTANT TRAIL DETAILS

OBSERVANCES (views, nature, wildlife…)

TRAIL SURFACE

EXPOSURE

NOTES FOR NEXT TIME

HIKING NOTES

ADVENTURE
is
calling

HIKING LOGBOOK

DATE: RATING: ☆☆☆☆☆

TRAIL	ELEVATION GAIN	LOSS
LOCATION		

DISTANCE	DURATION	START TIME	END TIME

TRAIL TYPE	DIFFICULTY	WEATHER	

IMPORTANT TRAIL DETAILS		OBSERVANCES (views, nature, wildlife...)	

TRAIL SURFACE	EXPOSURE	NOTES FOR NEXT TIME	

HIKING NOTES

ADVENTURE
awaits

HIKING LOGBOOK

DATE: RATING: ☆☆☆☆☆

TRAIL	ELEVATION GAIN	LOSS
LOCATION		

DISTANCE	DURATION	START TIME	END TIME

TRAIL TYPE	DIFFICULTY	WEATHER

IMPORTANT TRAIL DETAILS	OBSERVANCES (views, nature, wildlife...)

TRAIL SURFACE	EXPOSURE	NOTES FOR NEXT TIME

HIKING NOTES

HIKING LOGBOOK

DATE: RATING: ☆☆☆☆☆

TRAIL	ELEVATION GAIN	LOSS
LOCATION		

DISTANCE	DURATION	START TIME	END TIME

TRAIL TYPE	DIFFICULTY	WEATHER	

IMPORTANT TRAIL DETAILS		OBSERVANCES (views, nature, wildlife...)	

TRAIL SURFACE	EXPOSURE	NOTES FOR NEXT TIME	

HIKING NOTES

HIKING LOGBOOK

DATE

RATING: ☆☆☆☆☆

TRAIL	ELEVATION GAIN	LOSS

LOCATION

DISTANCE	DURATION	START TIME	END TIME

TRAIL TYPE	DIFFICULTY	WEATHER

IMPORTANT TRAIL DETAILS	OBSERVANCES (views, nature, wildlife...)

TRAIL SURFACE	EXPOSURE	NOTES FOR NEXT TIME

HIKING NOTES

ADVENTURE
is
calling

HIKING LOGBOOK

DATE:

RATING: ☆☆☆☆☆

TRAIL	ELEVATION GAIN	LOSS
LOCATION		

DISTANCE	DURATION	START TIME	END TIME

TRAIL TYPE	DIFFICULTY	WEATHER

IMPORTANT TRAIL DETAILS	OBSERVANCES (views, nature, wildlife...)

TRAIL SURFACE	EXPOSURE	NOTES FOR NEXT TIME

HIKING NOTES

ADVENTURE
awaits

HIKING LOGBOOK

DATE: RATING: ☆☆☆☆☆

TRAIL	ELEVATION GAIN	LOSS
LOCATION		

DISTANCE	DURATION	START TIME	END TIME

TRAIL TYPE	DIFFICULTY	WEATHER	

IMPORTANT TRAIL DETAILS	OBSERVANCES (views, nature, wildlife…)

TRAIL SURFACE	EXPOSURE	NOTES FOR NEXT TIME

HIKING NOTES

HIKING LOGBOOK

DATE: RATING: ☆☆☆☆☆

TRAIL		ELEVATION GAIN	LOSS
LOCATION			

DISTANCE	DURATION	START TIME	END TIME

TRAIL TYPE	DIFFICULTY	WEATHER	

IMPORTANT TRAIL DETAILS		OBSERVANCES (views, nature, wildlife…)	

TRAIL SURFACE	EXPOSURE	NOTES FOR NEXT TIME	

HIKING NOTES

LET'S
WANDER

HIKING LOGBOOK

DATE

RATING: ☆☆☆☆☆

TRAIL	ELEVATION GAIN	LOSS
LOCATION		

DISTANCE	DURATION	START TIME	END TIME

TRAIL TYPE	DIFFICULTY	WEATHER	

IMPORTANT TRAIL DETAILS	OBSERVANCES (views, nature, wildlife…)

TRAIL SURFACE	EXPOSURE	NOTES FOR NEXT TIME

HIKING NOTES

ADVENTURE
is
calling

HIKING LOGBOOK

DATE: RATING: ☆☆☆☆☆

TRAIL	ELEVATION GAIN	LOSS
LOCATION		

DISTANCE	DURATION	START TIME	END TIME

TRAIL TYPE	DIFFICULTY	WEATHER

IMPORTANT TRAIL DETAILS	OBSERVANCES (views, nature, wildlife…)

TRAIL SURFACE	EXPOSURE	NOTES FOR NEXT TIME

HIKING NOTES

ADVENTURE
awaits

HIKING LOGBOOK

DATE: RATING: ☆☆☆☆☆

TRAIL	ELEVATION GAIN	LOSS
LOCATION		

DISTANCE	DURATION	START TIME	END TIME

TRAIL TYPE	DIFFICULTY	WEATHER

IMPORTANT TRAIL DETAILS	OBSERVANCES (views, nature, wildlife...)

TRAIL SURFACE	EXPOSURE	NOTES FOR NEXT TIME

HIKING NOTES

HIKING LOGBOOK

DATE: RATING: ☆☆☆☆☆

TRAIL		ELEVATION GAIN	LOSS
LOCATION			

DISTANCE	DURATION	START TIME	END TIME

TRAIL TYPE	DIFFICULTY	WEATHER	

IMPORTANT TRAIL DETAILS	OBSERVANCES (views, nature, wildlife…)

TRAIL SURFACE	EXPOSURE	NOTES FOR NEXT TIME

HIKING NOTES

LET'S
WANDER

HIKING LOGBOOK

DATE   RATING: ☆ ☆ ☆ ☆ ☆

TRAIL	ELEVATION GAIN	LOSS
LOCATION		

DISTANCE	DURATION	START TIME	END TIME

TRAIL TYPE	DIFFICULTY	WEATHER

IMPORTANT TRAIL DETAILS	OBSERVANCES (views, nature, wildlife...)

TRAIL SURFACE	EXPOSURE	NOTES FOR NEXT TIME

HIKING NOTES

ADVENTURE
is
calling

HIKING LOGBOOK

DATE: RATING: ☆☆☆☆☆

TRAIL	ELEVATION GAIN	LOSS
LOCATION		

DISTANCE	DURATION	START TIME	END TIME

TRAIL TYPE	DIFFICULTY	WEATHER

IMPORTANT TRAIL DETAILS	OBSERVANCES (views, nature, wildlife...)

TRAIL SURFACE	EXPOSURE	NOTES FOR NEXT TIME

HIKING NOTES

ADVENTURE
awaits

HIKING LOGBOOK

DATE: RATING: ☆☆☆☆☆

TRAIL	ELEVATION GAIN	LOSS
LOCATION		

DISTANCE	DURATION	START TIME	END TIME

TRAIL TYPE	DIFFICULTY	WEATHER	

IMPORTANT TRAIL DETAILS		OBSERVANCES (views, nature, wildlife...)	

TRAIL SURFACE	EXPOSURE	NOTES FOR NEXT TIME	

HIKING NOTES

HIKING LOGBOOK

DATE: RATING: ☆☆☆☆☆

TRAIL	ELEVATION GAIN	LOSS
LOCATION		

DISTANCE	DURATION	START TIME	END TIME

TRAIL TYPE	DIFFICULTY	WEATHER	

IMPORTANT TRAIL DETAILS		OBSERVANCES (views, nature, wildlife…)	

TRAIL SURFACE	EXPOSURE	NOTES FOR NEXT TIME	

HIKING NOTES

LET'S
WANDER

Disclaimer and Copyright Notification:
Copyright © 2019 by Loveable Books / Julia Stüber
Julia Stüber
Eschersheimer Landstraße 42
60322 Frankfurt am Main
Germany

ISBN: 9781099972096

The contents in this book are based on the author's personal experience and research. Your results may vary, and will be based on your individual situation and motivation. There are no guarantees concerning the level of success you may experience. Your individual success depends on your motivation, dedication, background and desire.

70746594R00076

Made in the USA
Middletown, DE
27 September 2019